Published by Stratford Living Publishing.
ISBN Print: 978-1-990332-48-7

Dedicated to Gracie

This is a book about sheep,,,

An ewe is a lady sheep.

The word

EWE...

Rhymes with

YOU!

But you're not a sheep..
Or are you?

What's different between a ewe and you, you ask?

You can be a shepherd and lead sheep.

But no one can knit a sweater out of you!

So now it's time to ask you to...

JUMP JUMP JUMP AND ASK IS IT YOU OR EWE?

When we can't sleep we count sheep..

I wonder if sheep count us, when they can't sleep?

A gentleman sheep...

Is called a Ram.

But rams can't play football...

Or can they?

Aries

means RAM in Latin.

It's your star sign...

If you were born between March 21st and April 19th..

And now it's time to ask you to...

JUMP JUMP JUMP AND ASK IS IT YOU OR EWE?

A baby sheep is called a lamb,

Lambs are soft and cuddly and cute!

Sheep are clever animals!

They can solve puzzles...

Maybe even juggle?

A sheep can tell if you are smiling.

Or frowning...

Like us they prefer smiles!

So now it's time get ready to ask you to...

JUMP JUMP JUMP

AND ASK IS IT YOU OR EWE?

WE

EWE!

Other books in the
Jump Series:

Jump Like a Caribou!
Jump Like a Kangaroo!
Jump at the Zoo!
Jump and Say P.U.!
Jump and Say Boo!
Jump and Say Valentine's Day Is
For Kids Too!
Jump and Look For a Clue
Jump and Say Happy Birthday to
You!
Jump For Everything Blue!
Jump and Say Cock-A-Doodle-Do!

Jump and Squawk Like a Cockatoo!
Jump and Say There's an Ewww in My Stew!
Jump and Cheer Happy New Year!
Jump, Hop and Say Happy Easter To You!
Jump and Say There's A Moo-Moo in A Tutu!
Jump and Say There's A Hare in My Hair!
Jump and Say My Aunt Ate An Ant!

The Three Boulders
Billy Shakespeare
Billie Shakespeare

NON-FICTION
103 Fundraising Ideas For Parent Volunteers With Schools and Teams